# Seeing Stars

By Jill Atkins



Published in 2026 by
**Norwood House Press**
2544 Clinton Street
Buffalo, NY 14224



Printed in the United States of America

Library of Congress Cataloging-in-Publication Data:
Names: Atkins, Jill (Children's author). | Jones, Cath, 1965-, author. | Fernandez, Lidia, illustrator.
Title: Seeing stars / written by Jill Atkins. Floating / written by Cath Jones, illustrated by Lidia Fernandez.
Description: Buffalo, NY : Norwood House Press, 2026. | Series: Phonics all-stars: phase 4 |
Identifiers: ISBN 9781978578531 (pbk.) | ISBN 9781978578548 (library bound) | ISBN 9781978578555 (ebook)
Subjects: LCSH: Reading–Phonetic method–Juvenile fiction. | English language–Phonetics–Juvenile fiction. | Stars–Juvenile fiction. | Astronomy–Juvenile fiction. | Constellations–Juvenile fiction. | Weightlessness–Juvenile fiction. | Flight–Juvenile fiction. | Airplanes–Juvenile fiction.
Classification: LCC LB1573.3 A796 2026 | DDC 372.465–dc23

CPSIA compliance information: Batch #CW26NHP: For further information contact Norwood House Press at 1-800-237-9932.

Starlight is fantastic!

To see the stars, you need a clear, dark night with no moon.

You must stand as far from lights as you can.

Look up!

Can you see hundreds and hundreds of stars?

They are so clear and bright.

They seem to be glinting and flickering in the darkness.

With luck, you might see some shooting stars too.

Look! There is one. Do not blink or you will miss it.

Some stars you can see are in fact not stars at all. They are planets!

Stars are distant from us, but planets are near.

This is Mars, the red planet.

Some stars seem to form patterns.

This cluster of stars looks like a hunter.

This one looks like twins. Or do you see a dog? Or a pair of goats?

You must join the dots to see a pattern.

Do you think this looks like a cooking pan?

It is the Big Dipper.

Some stars are brighter than the rest.

If you sail on a ship, the bright stars can help you get back to land.

See if you can spot some of the patterns on a clear, dark night.

**This** might help you see them better!

# Floating

Written by
Cath Jones

Illustrated by
Lidia Fernandez

Josh and Amber were hanging out in the street.

“Win a fun, parabolic flight!” said a man.

“What is that?” said Josh.

“It is a sort of flight in a jet,” said the man. “It is terrific fun.”

“Boring!” said Josh. “My mom has a jet. I have been on loads of flights.”

Scrunch, scrunch. He put the booklet in the can.

"I might win," Amber said to the man.
"Can I have one ticket?"

Amber got herself a ticket.

She did win!

"You will need to check in at the airport," said the man. "Desk number seven."

At the airport, Amber sprang into the jet.

“Strap in tight,” said the man.

The jet took off. It was so quick that Amber felt helpless.

Then, as the jet fell back down, Amber felt odd.

She went up into the air!

"I can float!" Amber said.

"That is parabolic flight. You are floating in the air," said the man.

As the jet went up
and down, so did Amber.

Back on land, when Amber got out of the jet, she ran up to Josh.

“Parabolic flight is so much fun. We were all floating as the jet fell down,” Amber said.

Josh hid his disappointment. His mom's jet did not do parabolic flights.

What a bummer!